A GUIDE
TO
THE LAW OF CONTRACT
Ronald Skinner

Easyway Guides

Straightforward Publishing
Brighton BN2 4EG

ISBN 1900694 48 4

Cover design by Straightforward Graphics

Printed in England by CATS Solutions Swindon Wilts

Contents

Introduction

This latest book in the Easyway Guides Guide to The Law of Contract, Revised Edition, is a comprehensive and easy to understand introduction to the complex area of contract law.

Many people, either knowingly or unknowingly, enter into contracts without fully understanding the implications of what they are doing. Contracts can cover a number of areas, from hire purchase agreements to more complex finance agreements, contracts for construction of buildings, contracts for work around the house or contracts to supply goods.

Notwithstanding the type of contract or what area of life it relates to, there is a comprehensive framework of law, both in statute and also common law, which covers parties to a contract. This book will enable the reader, whether layperson or professional, to obtain the basic facts about contract law and also to see clearly where they stand in relation to their rights and obligations. Throughout the book there is reference to relevant court cases.

The book covers, amongst other areas:

- contracts and the law generally
- the formation of a contract
- the terms of a contract
- Implied terms
- misrepresentation
- remedies if a contract is breached.

A basic understanding of contracts will prove invaluable to any person who takes the time to understand more. This brief book will enable the reader to obtain that basic understanding.

Ronald Skinner 2006

1

The Making of a Contract

Underpinning all contracts there are four main principles:

1) A contract is an agreement between the parties to that contract-one person makes an offer and the other accepts that offer

2) Both parties have an intention to be legally bound by the agreement-this is usually known as an intention to create legal relations

3) Parties to the agreement need to be absolutely clear as to the terms of the agreement – this is the main area of contention with contracts, as we will see later

4) There must be consideration provided by each of the parties to the contract – this means that one person promises to give or deliver and the other promises to pay. The offer and the payment – either monetary or in kind - is the consideration.

When making a contract, or entering into a contract all parties to the contract must have the legal capacity to enter into a contract. Very importantly, a contract, in most cases, does not have to be in writing – a piece of paper is not necessary, the agreement and evidence of that agreement forms the basis of contract. We will outline those contracts which do need to be in writing later on in this chapter.

The nature of contracts – unilateral and bilateral contracts

The majority of contracts entered into are known as bilateral contracts. This quite simply means that each party to a contract agrees to take on an obligation. This obligation is underpinned by a promise to give something to the other party. A unilateral contract will arise where one party to the contract will make a promise to do something (usually to pay a sum of money) if the other party carries out a certain task. Examples of this are where you might undertake to pay someone a sum of money if they shave off their hair for charity or give up smoking. Estate agents enter into unilateral contracts whereby a percentage of sales go to the agent if they sell the property. However, the agent is not legally bound to sell the property, just to try to sell it.

The notion of offer and acceptance

As we have seen, for a contract to have legal status, usually one of the parties to the contract must have made an offer and the other party must have accepted the offer. Once the contract is accepted the agreement will be legally binding

The person making the offer is called the offeror and the person to whom the offer is made is known as the offeree. An offer may be express or implied. Express means that there is an express intention to offer goods and for X to pay an amount for the goods. Implied may mean, for example, when purchasing something from a store. The act of taking goods to a checkout means that there is an implied offer to buy those goods.

When dealing with contracts, or the formation of a contract most offers are made to specific parties. However, offers can also be made to a group of people or to the public at large. One such example is where a reward is offered to information following a crime.

One famous case dealing with offers to the public at large is Carlill v Carbolic Smokeball (1893) the defendants in this case were the manufacturers of 'smokeballs' popular at the time, which they claimed could prevent flu. They published adverts to this effect stating that anyone using their smoke balls and not being cured of flu would receive £100.

One person buying their smokeballs was a Mrs Carlill. It did not work and she claimed the £100. The manufacturers argument was to claim that their advert did not constitute a contract, since it was impossible to contract with the whole wide world. They claimed that they were not legally bound to pay the money. The court, needless to say, rejected this argument, which held that the advert did contract with the world. Mrs Carlill accepted the offer and duly claimed the £100. A contract such as the one above is usually a unilateral contract.

The invitation to treat
Certain kinds of transactions between parties might involve a preliminary stage where one party to the contract invites the other party to make an offer. This preliminary stage is known as 'invitation to treat'. One such case that demonstrates this is that of Gibson v Manchester City Council (1979). In this case, a council tenant of Manchester City Council expressed an interest in buying their house. The application was duly completed and sent to the council. A letter was received from the council stating that it may be prepared to sell the house to the tenant for £2180. The tenant, Mr Gibson, queried the purchase price pointing out that the path to the house was in bad condition. The council refused to alter the price, stating that the valuation reflected the condition of the property and the current property market. Mr Gibson then wrote asking the council to continue with the sale.

Following a change in the control of the council, and a new political approach, it was decided to stop the sale of houses to tenants. Mr Gibson was informed that his application had been declined, notwithstanding the initial offer. Legal proceedings were brought against the council claiming that the letter received by Mr Gibson, with the offer of sale at a price, constituted a contract, and was an offer which he duly accepted. The House of Lords, however, ruled that the council had not made an offer, the letter stating the purchase price was merely one step in the negotiations for a contract and amounted only to an invitation to treat. Its purpose in the first instance was quite simply to invite the making of a formal application, amounting to an offer, from the tenant.

Offers of sale in shops

Goods in shop windows marked with a price are generally regarded as invitations to treat, rather than offers to actually sell the goods at the price displayed. Where goods are sold on a self-service basis, the customer will make an offer to purchase on presenting the goods at the till and the shopkeeper may reject or accept that offer. One case which highlights this was Pharmaceutical Society of Great Britain v Boots Cash Chemists (Southern) Limited 1953. Boots were charged with an offence concerning the sale of items, medicines that could only be sold under the supervision of a qualified pharmacist. Two customers in a self-service shop selected the items, which were marked with a price from a shelf in the shop. The shelves were not supervised by a pharmacist but the pharmacist was instructed to supervise at the cash desk. The issue was whether the sale had taken place at the shelf or the cash desk. The Court of Appeal decided that the shelf display was like an advertisement and was therefore an invitation to treat. The offer was made by the customer when the items were placed in a basket and was only accepted when the

14

goods were taken to the cash desk. A pharmacist was supervising at that point so no offence was committed.

Following on from this principle, shops do not have to sell goods at the marked price and a customer cannot insist on buying a particular good on display. Displaying the goods is not an offer so a customer cannot accept it making a binding contract. (In reality, if shops do display goods at a price they generally sell it at that price although, as we have seen they do not have to).

Contracts and advertisements

A distinction is generally made between advertisements for unilateral contracts and advertisements for bilateral contracts. Advertisements for unilateral contracts will include those such as described in the case of Carlill and Carbolic Smokeball Co or those offering a reward for information or for lost property. They are usually treated as offers on the basis that no further negotiations are need between the parties to the offer and the person making the offer will usually be bound by it.

One recent case is that of Bowerman v Association of British Travel Agents Ltd (1996) in which a school had booked a skiing holiday with a travel agent, which was a member of ABTA. Any member of ABTA has to display a notice as follows:

Where holidays or other travel arrangements have not yet commenced at the time of failure of the tour operator, ABTA arranges for you to be reimbursed the money you have paid for your holiday.

In this case the tour operator became insolvent and all holidays were cancelled. The school was refunded the money paid for the holiday but not the cost of the travel insurance taken out, which was significant. The case was taken to court and ABTA lost because the notice constituted an offer which h the school accepted by contracting with the ABTA member.

Bilateral contracts

Bilateral contracts are the type which advertise specified goods at a certain price such as those found in shop windows and in magazines. They are usually considered invitations to treat on the grounds that they may lead to further bargaining. One such case which highlights this is Partridge v Crittendon (1968). An advertisement in a magazine stated 'Bramblefinch cocks and hens 25shillings each'. As the Bramblefinch was a protected species, the person who placed the advert was charged with unlawfully offering for sale a wild bird which was against the Protection of Birds Act 1954, but the conviction was quashed on the grounds that the advertisement was not an offer but an invitation to treat.

The length of time an offer should last

An offer may cease to exist in any of the following circumstances:

Where an offeror states that an offer will be open for a specified time

Where the offeror has not specified how long the offer will remain open, the offer will lapse after a reasonable length of time has passed. How much time can be deemed reasonable will depend on whether the offer was communicated quickly and also on the subject matter.

Some offers are made subject to certain specified conditions, and if these conditions are not in place, the offer may lapse.

An offer may lapse if and when the offeree rejects it. For

example if A offers to sell B a car on Tuesday, and B says no, B cannot come back on Wednesday and insist on accepting the offer

A counter offer can terminate the original offer. One case that highlights this is Hyde v Wrench (1840) where the defendant offered to sell his farm for £1000 and the plaintiff responded by offering to buy it at £950-this is termed making a counter offer. The farm owner refused to sell at that price and when the plaintiff later tried to buy the farm at £1000, the original asking price, it was held that this offer was no longer available. The counter offer had terminated the original offer

The death of the offeror can affect the offer. If the offeree knows of the death of the offeror then the offer is terminated. If they did not the offer still stands, although this is one area of law that is still unclear. It very much depends on the circumstances at the time

An offer may be revoked, withdrawn, at any time until it has been accepted. This is the basic rule, although there are a number of other principles. It is not enough for an offeror simply to change his or her mind about an offer. The offeror must notify the offeree that the offer has been revoked. Revocation does not specifically have to be communicated by the offeror, it can be by another reliable party.

Acceptance of an offer

Acceptance of an offer must be unconditional, accepting the precise terms of the offer. Where the process of negotiation is long and difficult, it might be difficult to pinpoint exactly when an offer has been made and accepted. In such cases a court will examine the precise course of negotiations to ascertain whether the parties have reached agreement, if at all and when. This process can be complicated when the so-called 'battle of forms' occurs. Rather than negotiating terms each time a contract is made many companies try to use standard conditions, which will be printed on headed stationary, such as order forms and delivery notes. The 'battle of forms' occurs when one party sends a form stating that the contract is on their terms, and the other party responds by sending back the forms and stating that the contract is on their terms. The general rule in these cases is that the 'last shot' wins the battle. Each new form issued is treated as a counter offer, so that when one party performs its obligation under the contract the action will be seen as acceptance by the other side. One simple case that illustrates this is British Road Services v Crutchley (Arthur V) Ltd (1968), the plaintiffs delivered some whisky to the defendants for storage. The BRS driver handed the defendants a delivery note, which listed the company's terms of carriage. The note was accepted and stamped with Crutchleys terms and conditions and the court held that by accepting this, the BRS driver had accepted a counter offer. Although many cases are simple, other more recent case law has held that the last shot will not always succeed.

It is a basic assumption that there is no acceptance until the act has been thoroughly performed. However, in some cases, part performance may amount to acceptance. In Errington v Errington (1952) a father bought a house in his own name for £750, borrowing £500 of the price from a building society. He bought the house for his son and daughter in law to live in, and told them that they must meet the mortgage repayments. If they met the payments the house would be signed over to them on completion of the term. The couple moved in and began to pay the mortgage, but they never in fact made the promise to continue with the payments until the mortgage was paid off, which meant that the contract was unilateral.

When the father later died, the people in charge of his affairs sought to withdraw the offer. The Court of Appeal held that it was too late to do this. The part performance of the son and daughter in law constituted an acceptance of the contract and the father and his representatives after death were bound by the resulting contract unless the son and daughter in law ceased the payments, in which case the offer was no longer binding.

A request for information about an offer does not constitute a counter offer, so the original offer remains open.

If an offeree has to accept an offer in a specified manner, then only acceptance by that method or an equally effective one will be binding

Communicating acceptance of an offer

An acceptance will not usually take effect until it is clearly communicated to the offeror. However, there are some circumstances where acceptance may take effect without it being communicated to the offeror. An offer may clearly state, or indeed imply, that acceptance need not be communicated to the offeror. An offeror who fails to receive an acceptance through their own fault may be prevented from claiming that the non-communication means they should not be bound by the contract.

The general rule for acceptances by post is that they take effect when they are posted, rather than when they are communicated. The postal rule was laid down in the case of Adams v Lindsell (1818), when on the 2nd of September 1817, the defendants wrote to the plaintiffs, who were in the wool processing business, offering to sell them a quantity of sheep fleeces, and stating that they required an answer 'in course of post'. However, the defendants did not address the letter correctly and it did not reach the plaintiffs until the evening of September the 5th. The plaintiffs posted their acceptance the same evening, and it reached the defendants on the

9th of September. If the original letter had been correctly addressed it would have reached the plaintiffs by the 7th of September. Because it was incorrectly addressed it did not and no reply was received and the wool was sold to a third party. The issue was whether a sale had been made before the sale of the wool to the third party. The court heard that the contract was concluded as soon as the acceptance was posted and that the defendants were bound from the evening of 5th September so should not have sold the wool to a third party.

There are certain exceptions to the postal rule. The offeror may avoid the postal rule by making it a specific term of their offer that acceptance will only take effect when it is communicated to them.

Ignorance of the offer

It is generally accepted that a person cannot accept an offer of which they are unaware, because in order to create a binding contract, the parties must reach agreement. This is a very important principle.

Tenders, auctions and the sale of land

The rules outlined above also apply to the sale of land and to sales by tender and auction.

Tenders

If a large organization, such as a company or government department needs to contract a supplier of goods or services, it will, more often than not, advertise for tenders, i.e., bids. Organizations wishing to supply goods or services will reply, detailing price for these services. The advertiser will choose from the replies. And contact the successful tenderer.

As a general rule, the request for tenders is regarded as an invitation to treat (see previous) so there is no specific obligation to accept any of the tenders sent. The tenders themselves are offers and a contract does not come into existence until one is accepted.

In some cases however, an invitation for tenders may in itself be an offer. The main example of this is where the invitation to tender makes it clear that the lowest tender (or highest) will be accepted.

The implications of choosing to accept a tender depend on what sort of tender is involved.

Specific tenders

Where an invitation to tender specifies that a particular quantity of goods is required on a particular date, or between certain dates, agreeing to one of the tenders submitted will constitute acceptance of an offer, creating a contract between the parties.

Non-specific tenders

Some invitations to tender are not specific, and may for example simply state that certain goods may be required, up to a particular maximum quantity, with deliveries to be made if and when requested. For example, an invitation to tender made by a hospital may ask for tenders to supply goods, if and when required. In this case, taking up one of the tenders submitted does not amount to acceptance of an offer in the contractual sense and there is no contract. The hospital may take the goods all at one, some at a time or none at all. It is not bound.

Auction sales

The parties to an auction sale are the bidder and the owner of the goods. The auctioneer supplies a service and is not party to the contract between buyer and seller.

Sale of land

The standard rules of contract apply to the sale of land, including buildings. However, the court applies the rules strictly in the case of land, tending to require very clear evidence of an intention to be bound before they will state that an offer has been made. In Harvey v Facey (1893) the plaintiffs sent the defendants a telegram asking 'will you sell us Bumper Hall Pen? Telegraph lowest cash price'. The reply arrived back stating 'Lowest price for Bumper Hall pen £900'. The plaintiffs then sent a telegram saying 'we agree to buy Bumper Hall Pen for £900. Please send us your title deeds'. On these facts, the Privy Council held that there was no contract. They regarded the telegram from the defendants as a statement of price only. It was therefore not an offer which could be accepted by the third telegram.

In practice there are rigid procedures involved in the sale of land. The first is the 'sale subject to contract', where the parties agree to the sale and the implication is that there is a good deal of proving and other work before a contract is in existence. The next stage is the exchange of contract, where the buyer and seller agree to the terms of the formal contract. Once the contracts are exchanged then the contract is binding and any backing out can result in a claim for damages and lost deposit.

Certainty of contract

In order to be viewed as a binding contract, an agreement must be absolutely certain. that is it should not be vague or incomplete. One such case that amplifies this is that of Scammell v Ouston (1941) where the parties agreed that Ouston could buy a van from Scammell, giving his lorry in part exchange paying the balance over two-years on hire purchase terms. Scammell decided to back out and claimed that there was no contract between the parties. The

House of Lords Agreed, pointing out that the courts would uphold an agreement if there really was one, in this case the terms were too vague, particularly the agreement to pay on Hire Purchase Terms.

In certain cases, parties may leave details vague, particularly when dealing with fluctuating prices and other factors. Provisions should be in the contract stating how they should be clarified.

Terms implied into contract by statute

In some cases, statute will override contract and will provide that certain provisions should be read into contracts even though they have not been specifically agreed between the parties. For example, under the Sale of Goods act 1979 an agreement for the sale of goods can become binding as soon as the parties have agreed to buy and sell, with the details of the contract being laid down by law, or determined by the standard of reasonableness. In such a case, the parties do not even have had to agree on a price. The buyer is entitled to pay a reasonable price. Terms implied by statute will be examined further on in this book.

Intention to create legal relations

One major principle of contract law is that of intention to create legal relations. If two or more parties make an agreement without the intention of being legally bound by it, the agreement will not be regarded as a contract.

As far as intent to be legally bound is concerned, contracts can be divided into domestic and social agreements on one hand, and commercial agreements on the other. Where the agreement falls into the former category there is an assumption that the parties do not intend to create legal relations. The reverse is true when it comes to commercial agreements.

Domestic and social agreements

Where a husband and wife who are living together as one household make an agreement, the courts will assume that they do not intend to be legally bound, unless the agreement states other wise. In Balfour v Balfour (1919) the defendant was a civil servant stationed in Sri Lanka. While the couple were on leave in England, Mrs. Balfour was taken ill, and it became clear that her husband would have to return by himself. He promised to pay her maintenance of £30 per month. They eventually separated and the husband refused to make any more payments. The Court of Appeal decided he was not bound to make further payments, as when the agreement was made there was no intention to create legal relations.

Likewise, agreements between parents and children are assumed not to be legally binding.

Social agreements

The presumption that an agreement is not intended to be legally binding is also applied to social relationships between people who are not related. With both the above though, there can be exceptions.

Commercial agreements

There is a storing presumption in commercial agreements that the parties intend to be legally bound, and unless clear words are used this presumption stands. Where the words of a business agreement are ambiguous, the courts will favor the interpretation which suggests that the parties did intend to create legal relations.

The capacity to enter into a contract

There are categories of people in society whose power to make contracts is limited by law. The main categories are minors and people considered incapable of contracting due to mental disorders or some other condition of incapacity such as drunkenness or under influence of certain drugs.

In addition, the contracting capacity of a company or corporation will also have a bearing, i.e. the legal capacity to enter into a contract in the first place.

The basic common law rule is that contracts do not bind minors. In some cases however, as in much of contract law, there are contracts that will bind minors. The main contracts binding on a minor are contracts to supply 'necessaries'. Under the Sale of Goods Act 1979, necessaries means 'goods suitable to the condition in life of the minor or other person concerned and to his actual requirements at the time of sale and delivery'. When deciding if a contract is one for necessaries, the courts first of all determine whether the goods or services are capable of amounting to necessaries in law, and then consider whether they are necessary for the minor in question.

Mental incapacity

This category covers people who suffer from mental disability, and those who are drunk when the contract is made. In general terms, contracts made with people in either state will be valid unless, very importantly, at the time the contract was made, the person is incapable of understanding the nature of the transaction and the other party knows this. In such circumstances, the contract is voidable. The party suffering the disability can choose to void it.

Where one party is incapable, through disability as described, of understanding the nature of the contract, but the other party is unaware, the courts will ignore the disability. One important case highlighting this is Hart v O'Connor (1985) the Privy Council held that a person of unsound mind was bound by his agreement to sell some land because when the contract was made the buyer did not realize that the buyer had any mental incapacity.

The fact also that language may be a barrier does not render a person incapable of making a contract.

Corporations

A corporation is a legal entity which is treated by law as having a separate identity from the persons who constitute it. There are three main types of corporation: registered companies, corporations established by statute and chartered corporations. Each has a different level of contracting ability.

Registered companies

These are companies registered under the Companies act 1985 – most commercial companies. When registering, companies must supply a document which regulates their activities called a memorandum of association, which contains information including an objects clause, laying down the range of activities which their company can engage in.

Under the 1989 Act a company can be liable for a contract made outside its stated activities if the other party has acted in good faith.

Statutory companies

These corporations are created by an Act of Parliament for specific purposes, the Independent Broadcasting Authority is an example, as are local authorities. The statute creating the particular corporation will specify the purposes for which that corporation may make contracts.

Any contracted outside of these purposes is null and void.

Chartered corporations

These are corporations set up by Royal Charter, which means that their rights are officially granted by the Crown, examples are charities and some universities and other educational institutions. They have the same contractual capacity as an adult human being.

Formalities

We have discussed the fact that an agreement does not have to take a specific written form in order to be deemed a binding contract. A contract can be oral. One famous recent case involving an oral contract was Hadley v Kemp where Gary Kemp was the songwriter in the group Spandau Ballet. He was sued by other members of then group for royalties received for the group's music. The basis of the claim was that there was an oral agreement to share royalties. They were unable to prove the existence of any oral agreement and their claim failed.

Contracts which must be made by deed

The Law of Property Act 1925 states that a contract for a lease of more than three years must be made by deed, which basically means that it must be put into a formal document, signed in front of witnesses.

Contracts which must be in writing

Some statutes lay down that certain types of contract must be in writing. Most contracts involving sales of land must be in writing, under the Law of Property Act 1989. Other contracts that need to be in writing are those involving the transfers of shares in a limited company (Companies Act 1985), bills of exchange; cheques and promissory notes (Bills of Exchange Act (1882); and regulated consumer credit agreements, such as hire purchase agreements (Consumer Credit Act 1974).

Contracts, which must be evidenced in writing

Contracts of guarantee (where one party guarantees the obligations of another, such as parents guaranteeing a sons or daughters overdraft) are required to be 'evidenced in writing'. Contracts for sale or disposition of land before 27th September 1989 are still covered by the old law Prior to the Law of Property act 1989.

Evidenced in writing means that although the contract itself may not be a written one, there must be written evidence of the transaction. The evidence must have existed before one party tried to enforce the contract against the other, and it must be signed by the party against whom the contract is to be enforced.

Main points from chapter one

Underpinning all contracts there are four main principles:

- A contract is an agreement between the parties to that contract – one person makes an offer and the other accepts that offer

- Both parties have an intention to be legally bound by the agreement – this is usually known as an intention to create legal relations

- Parties to the agreement have to be very clear as to the terms of the agreement

- There must be consideration provided by each of the parties to the contract.

Other aspects of contracts are:

- Contracts do not have to be in writing

- A contract must be clear and certain in its intent

- People must have the capacity to enter into an agreement

2

Consideration and Contracts

As we saw in chapter 1, English law states that a contract is not usually binding unless it is supported by consideration. Consideration is usually said to mean that each party to a contract must give something in return for what is gained from the other party. Very basically, if there is a dispute and you wish to enforce someone's promise to you must prove that you gave something in return for that promise.

Consideration may be goods or services, a thing or a service. Many problems concerning consideration arise not when a contract is made but when one or other of the parties to the contract seeks to modify it, such as paying a lower price than agreed or supplying a different good or service.

Promisor and promisee

In most contracts, it is the case that two promises will be exchanged, so each party to the contract is promisor and promisee. In a contract case, the claimant will often be arguing that the defendant has broken the promise made to the claimant and therefore the claimant will usually be the promisee. One example is if A contracts to build a conservatory and B promises to pay £5000 for the conservatory, there are two promises in this contract. A's promise to build a conservatory and B's promise to pay. If A fails to build the conservatory B can sue him. If the issue of consideration arises, B will seek to prove that his promise to pay £5000 was consideration for A's promise for building the conservatory. In that action, A will be the promisor and B the promisee. However, reverse the situation and B fails to pay, then A will sue and, if consideration is at issue, A will have to prove that his promise to build the conservatory was consideration for B's promise to pay. In that action, A will be the promisee and B the promisor.

'Executory' and 'executed' consideration

Consideration can fall into two categories: executory and executed. Executed consideration is the performance of an act in return for a promise. Executory consideration is when the defendant makes a promise, and the plaintiff offers a counter promise – you promise to deliver goods to me and I promise to pay for them when they arrive, the promise is executory because it is something to be done in the future.

Consideration must be given in return for the promise or act of the other party. Something done, given, or promised beforehand will not be counted as consideration. A classic case concerning this arose in Roscords v Thomas (1842). The defendant sold the plaintiff a horse. After the sale was completed, the defendant told the plaintiff that the animal was 'sound and free from any vice'. This was not the actual truth and the plaintiff sued. The court held that the defendants promise was unenforceable, because it was made after the sale. If the promise about the horse's condition had been made before, the plaintiff would have provided consideration for it by buying the horse. As it was made after the sale, the consideration was past, for it had not been given in return for the promise.

There are two exceptions to the rule that past consideration is no consideration. The first is where the past consideration was provided at the promisors request, and it was understood that payment would be made. The second is the bill of exchange. Under s27 of the Bills of Exchange Act 1882, an 'antecedent debt or liability' may be consideration for receipt of a bill of exchange.

Consideration must be of economic value
What this principle basically means is that there must be some physical value, rather than just an emotional or sentimental value.

Consideration can be a promise not to sue
If one party has a possible civil claim against the other, a promise not to enforce that claim is good consideration for a promise given in return. One clear example is if A crashes into B's car then A can promise not to sue if B pays for the damage.

Performance of an existing duty
Where a promisee already owes the promisor a legal duty, then in theory performing that duty should not in itself be consideration. – if the promisee does nothing more than they are already obliged to do, they are suffering no detriment and the promisor is only getting a benefit to which he or she is entitled.

Existing duties can be divided into three categories: public duties; contractual duties to the promisor; and contractual duties to a third party.

Existing public duty
Where a person is merely carrying out duties they are legally bound to perform – such as police officer or juror, doing that alone will not be consideration. However, where a promisee is under a public duty, but does something beyond the call of that duty, that extra act amounts to consideration. In Glasbrook Brothers v Glamorgan County Council (1925) the owners of a South Wales Mine asked the

police to place a guard at their colliery during a strike. The police suggested that regular checks by mobile patrol would be adequate but the owners replied that they wanted something more intensive and the police agreed at an extra cost of £2,200. After the strike the owners refused to pay saying that the police had a duty to protect their property. The courts held in favor of the police saying that the police did not have a duty to supply the cover they did, only the cover they deemed sufficient. Anything over and above was deemed consideration.

Existing contractual duty to the promisor

The position on contractual duties and consideration has changed from the traditional position whereby the performance of an existing contractual duty owed to a promisor was not consideration. In Stilk v Myrick (1809) two sailors deserted a ship during a voyage and the captain was unable to find replacements. The remaining crew members were promised extra wages for sailing the ship back to London but the captain refused to pay on arrival and the sailors sued with the court holding that there was no consideration as the sailors had already contracted to sail the boat back to its destination. In Hartley v Ponsonby (1857) half the crew deserted and the remaining crew were offered extra wages to carry on the journey. At the end the captain refused to pay and the crew sued and won, as the courts held that there was consideration as the crew were to small to sail the boat adequately and extra money was justified.

Existing contractual duty to a third party

In some cases two parties make a contract to provide a benefit to a third party. If one of the parties (A) makes a further promise to that third party to provide the benefit they have already contracted to provide, that further promise can be good consideration for a

34

promise made by the third party in return-even though nothing more than the contractual duty is being promised by A. One case that illustrates this is Scotson v Pegg (1861). Scotson contracted to supply a cargo of coal to a third party, X, or to anyone X nominated. Sotson was instructed by X to deliver the coal to Pegg, and Pegg promised to unload the coal at a stated rate of pay. He subsequently failed to do the agreed unloading. Scotson sued Pegg, claiming that their promise to deliver coal to him was consideration for his promise to unload it. Peg claimed that this could not be consideration, since Scotson was already bound to supply the coal under the contract with X. The court upheld Scotsons claim: delivery of the coal was consideration because it was a benefit to Pegg, and a detriment to Scottson in that it prevented them from having the option of breaking their contract with X.

Waiver and promissory estoppel

These are ways of making some kind of promise binding even where there is no consideration. Waiver has traditionally applied where one party agrees not to enforce their strict rights under the contract by, for example, accepting delivery later than agreed. One case which illustrates the doctrine of waiver is that of Hickman v Haynes (1875). A buyer asked the seller to deliver goods later than originally agreed and then when the delivery was made refused to accept it. The seller sued for breach of contract, the buyer responded by arguing that the seller was in breach, for delivering later than specified. The courts rejected the buyer's argument on the ground s that the delivery was made at the buyer's request.

Promissory estoppel (stopping the contract on the basis of a promise) is a newer doctrine than waiver, developing the concept. This is illustrated by the case of Hughes v Metropolitan Railways Co (187) involving the landlord and his tenants. Under the lease, the tenants were obliged to keep the premises in good repair, and in October 1874, the landlord gave them six months notice to do some repairs stating that if they were not done in time, the lease would be forfeited. In November the two parties began to negotiate the possibility of the tenants buying the lease, the tenants stating in the meantime that they would not carry out the repairs. By December the negotiations had broken down and at the end of the six-month notice period, the landlord claimed that the lease was forfeited because the tenants had not done the repairs. The House of Lords held however, that the ;landlords conduct was an implied promise to the tenants that he would not enforce the forfeiture at the end of the notice period, and in not doing the repairs, the tenants had been relying on this premise. It was seen that the six-month notice period began again when negotiations broke down.

Agreement by deed

There is one other way in which a promise can be made binding without consideration.: it can be put into a document called a deed. An agreement by deed is often described as a 'formal' contract. Other types of contract are known as simple contracts. The procedure for making a contract by deed is laid down in s1 of the Law of Property (Miscellaneous Provisions) Act 1989 and usually involves signing a formal document in the presence of a witness. Deeds are usually used to give legal effect to what otherwise might be a gratuitous gift, which could be unenforceable for lack of consideration.

Main points from chapter two

- English law states that a contract is not usually binding unless it is supported by consideration

- Consideration is usually said to mean that each party to a contract must give something in return for what is gained from the other party

- Consideration may be goods or services, a thing or a service.

3

The Terms of a Contract

Terms of contracts describe the respective duties and obligations of each party to the contract. As well as the contractual terms laid out and agreed by parties to a contract, called express terms, there may also be implied terms – terms which are 'read into' a contract because of the facts of the agreement and the apparent intention of the parties or the law on specific types of contract.

Express terms of contract

Oral statements

In all transactions, with the exception of the simplest, there will be some negotiations before a contract is made. These are usually oral statements or based on oral statements. Problems can arise following oral statements when parties cannot agree whether the statement was intended to be binding. In considering questions such as these a court will classify statements made during negotiations as either representations or terms. A representation is a statement which may have encouraged one of the parties to make the contract but is not itself part of the contract, while a term is an undertaking that is part of the contract. Representation can also be construed as misrepresentation which is a common cause of dispute.

Whether a statement is either a representation or a term is mainly a question of the parties intentions, If the parties have indicated that a particular statement is a term of their contract, then the court will carry out that intention.

Written terms of a contract

Written terms can be incorporated into a contract in three different ways: by signature, by reasonable notice and by a previous course of dealing.

The parol evidence rule

Under this rule, where there is a written contract, extrinsic (parole) evidence cannot change the express terms laid down in that document. Extrinsic evidence includes oral statements and written material such as draft contracts or letter, whether relating to pre-contract negotiations or the parties post contractual behavior

One case that illustrates the parole evidence rule is Henderson v Arthur (1907). The plaintiffs and the defendant were parties to a lease which contained a covenant for the payment of rent quarterly in advance, although before the lease was drawn up the parties agreed that the rent could be paid in arrears. When the tenant was sued for not paying quarterly in advance, he pointed out this prior agreement. The court held that the terms of prior oral agreement could not be substituted for the terms of a later formal contract covering the same transaction. There are a few exceptions to the parol evidence rule, the following being the main ones:

Rectification

Where a document is intended to record a previous oral agreement but fails to do that accurately, evidence of the oral agreement will be admitted.

Partially written agreements

Where there is a written agreement, but the parties clearly intended it to be qualified by other written or oral statements, the parol evidence rule is displaced.

Implied terms

The parol evidence rule only applies where a party seeks to use existing evidence to alter the express terms of a contract. Where a contract is of a type that is unusually subject to terms implied by law, parol evidence may be given to support, or to deny, the usual implication.

Collateral agreements

There is a way in which an oral statement can be deemed binding, even though it conflicts with a written contract and does not fall within any of the exceptions to the parol rule. If one party says something like 'I will sign this document if you will assure me that it means....' The courts may find that two contracts have been created, the written agreement and a collateral contract based on the oral statement.

Construction of express terms in contracts

The courts will sometimes have to determine the construction of an express term within a contract. The courts will have to 'seek the meaning which the document would convey to a reasonable person having all the background knowledge which would have reasonably been available to parties at the time of entering into the agreement'. The courts start by presuming that the parties meant what they said. The courts would also look at the outcome of the words and meaning to see if they create an absurdity or are inconsistent with the rest of the contract.

Implied terms

As well as the express terms laid down in the contract, further terms may be sometimes read into the contract by the courts. These implied terms are divided into four groups: terms implied by fact, terms implied by law, terms implied by custom and terms implied by trade usage.

Terms implied by fact are terms not laid out in the contract, but which it is assumed both parties would have intended to include if they had thought about it, they may have left them out by mistake. In order to decide what the intention of the parties was the courts have developed two tests, the 'officious bystander test, and the 'business efficacy' test. The officious bystander test was laid down in Shirlaw v Southern Foundries (1926). The Judge said, ...'that which in any contract is left to be implied and need not be expressed is something so obvious that it goes without saying: so that, if while the parties were making their bargain, an officious bystander were to suggest some express provision for it in the agreement, they would testily suppress him with a common 'oh, of course'.

The business efficacy test covers terms which one side alleges must be implied to make the contract work, to give it business efficacy.

Terms implied by law are terms which the law dictates must be present in certain types of contract.-in some cases whether the parties intended them or not. In Liverpool Council v Irwin (1977) the defendants lived in a council maisonette which was part of a high rise block in Liverpool. The block was in a bad condition and tenants withheld rent and the case went to court with the tenants arguing that the council was in breach of contract. (tenancy). The council argued that there was no agreement to keep the block in good condition and the courts argued that good repair and safety were implied terms of contract. The council lost the case.

Terms implied by custom can be implied into a contract if there is evidence that under local custom they would normally be there.

Terms implied by trade usage would normally be part of a contract made by parties in a particular trade or business.

The importance of contractual terms

There are three types of contractual terms, conditions, warranties and innominate terms. A condition is a term which the courts would regard as important in that it would clearly have negative consequences if breached. Where a condition is breach the injured party can regard the contract as repudiated, and need not render any further performance, and can also sue for damages.. Warranties denote contractual terms which can be broken without highly important consequences. This would be a minor term and would not entitle the party to terminate the contract or sue. Inominate terms are terms which can be broken with either important or trivial consequences, depending on the nature of the breach. Inominate terms were illustrated in Hong Kong Fir Shipping Co Ltd v Kawasaki (1962) in which the defendants had chartered a ship for two years from the claimants. 20 weeks of the charter were lost due to condition of ship and incompetent staff. The agreement contained a clause stating that the ship was 'in every way fitted for ordinary cargo service'. There was no doubt that the defendants were entitled to bring an action for damages but instead decided to terminate the contract. The claimants counter sued, claiming that the breach did not entitle the defendants to terminate, only to claim damages. The Court of Appeal agreed, stating that the question to be asked was that whether as a result of the breach the defendants had been deprived of the whole of the benefit of the contract. As this was not the case, the termination was unjustified.

Unfair contract terms

Contract terms can be considered to be so unfair to one of the contracting parties that the courts have had to intervene to prevent an injustice. This has usually arisen within the context of exemption clauses and is controlled both by common law and the Unfair Contract Terms Act 1977. The European Union has also passed directives preventing unfair terms in contract.

Exemption clauses in contracts

In certain cases, one party to a contract may seek to avoid incurring liabilities for breach of contract, or may specify that their liability for such a breach will be limited, usually to a specific amount of damages. However, a clause which seeks to exclude all liability for uncertain breaches is called an exclusion clause. There are many examples such as holiday companies seeking to exclude all liability for holidays gone wrong or cancelled. Over the past 40 years the law has sought to control the use of these clauses, first by the efforts of judges and also by legislation such as the Unfair Contract Terms Act 1977 and the Unfair Terms in Consumer Contracts Regulations 1999.

Misrepresentation in contracts

Even in cases where a contract clearly meets the requirements of offer and acceptance, consideration and intent to create legal relations, it will still not be binding if, at the time the contract was made, certain factors were present which meant that there was no genuine concern. These are known as vitiating factors (because they vitiate, or invalidate, consent). The vitiating factors which the law recognizes as preventing a contract are misrepresentation, mistake, duress, undue influence and illegality.

Misrepresentation

If one party has been induced to enter into a contract by a

statement made by the other party, and that statement is untrue, the contract is voidable and the innocent party may also be able to claim damages. For a misrepresentation to be actionable it must be untrue, a statement of fact not opinion, and it must have induced the innocent party to enter into the contract. There are four different types of misrepresentation, fraudulent misrepresentation, where there is clear deceit, negligent, where misrepresentation arises through acts of negligence but not deceit and innocent misrepresentation which is not fraudulent but is still clear misrepresentation.

The effect of a misrepresentation is generally to make a contract voidable, rather than void, so the contract will continue to exist unless or until the injured party chooses to have it set aside by the courts by means of rescission.

Rescission is an equitable remedy which sets the contract aside and puts the parties back in the position where they were before the misrepresentation. An injured party who decides to rescind the contract may do so by notifying the other party or, if this is not possible owing to the conduct of the party, by taking some reasonable action to indicate the intention to default. A case that illustrates this is Car and Universal Finance Co Ltd v Caldwell (1965) where the defendant sold and delivered a car and was paid by cheque. The cheque bounced, by which time the car and buyer had disappeared. The defendant notified the police and the Automobile Association. While the police were investigating the buyer sold the car to a dealer who knew that the car was not the buyers to sell. Finally, the car dealer sold the car to the claimants who bought it in good faith. The court of Appeal held that by contacting the police and the AA the claimant had made his intention to rescind the contract clear. As soon as this happened the ownership of the car reverted to him. This meant that at the time the car was sold back to the claimant the car was not anyone's to sell.

Misrepresentation and terms

Section 1 of the Misrepresentation Act 1967 provides that where a misrepresentation becomes a term of the contract, the innocent party may bring an action for both misrepresentation and breach of contract. Under section 3 of this Act, as amended by the Unfair Contract Terms Act 1977, exemption clauses which attempt to exclude or limit liability for misrepresentations are operative only if reasonable. This provision is illustrated in Walker v Boyle (1982) where the seller of a house told the buyer that there were no disputes regarding the boundaries of the property. This was not true. This misrepresentation appeared to entitle the buyer to rescind the contract and notwithstanding a clause seeking to deny this, the court granted a rescission.

Main points from chapter three

- The terms of a contract describe the respective duties and obligations of each party to the contract

- As well as the contractual terms laid out and agreed by parties to a contract, called express terms, there may also be implied terms – terms which are 'read into' a contract because of the facts of the agreement and the apparent intentions of the parties or the law on specific types of contract

- Contracts can be considered to be so unfair to one of the contracting parties that the courts have had to intervene to prevent an injustice. The unfair Contract Terms Act 1977 along with common law will regulate this area

- Misrepresentation in contracts can render a contract voidable

4

Errors Affecting Parties to the Contract

In certain cases, a mistake within a contract can render that contract void. However, the law in this area operates quite rigidly.

The general principles

There are two types of mistake within contract law, Common mistake and cross-purpose mistake. Both are underpinned by general rules. There is an objective principle, or test which the court will apply when considering mistakes within contracts. The courts do not ask the parties to the contract what they thought they were entering into but rather they consider what an onlooker would have thought it was each party was agreeing to. This is very much akin to the 'officious bystander test' referred to earlier.

Another key principle is that in order to void a contract the mistake must be made before the contract is completed. One case that illustrates this is Amalgamated Investment and Property Co Ltd v John Walker and sons Ltd (1977). In this case, a contract was made for the sale of a warehouse, for £1,710,000. The sellers knew that the purchasers were buying the warehouse with the intention of redeveloping it.

The day after the contract was signed, the Department of the Environment, as it was then, made the property a listed building. This made it more difficult for the buyers to get permission to redevelop. Without this permission the warehouse would be worth considerably less. Neither party to the contract had been aware that the DOE were going to list the building.

The Court of Appeal held that the contract was valid as at the time of the agreement both parties were perfectly correct in their belief that the building was not listed, so there was no operative mistake.

In the past, only a mistake of fact could negate a contract not a mistake of law. However, in the light of certain key cases, this is not now the case.

Common mistake

Having explored the general principles underpinning the treatment of mistakes in contract it is now time to explore the two types of mistake more thoroughly.

Common mistakes are also known as identical mistakes, shared mistake or mistake nullifying consent. In this situation both parties make the same mistake-for example if A buys an antique from B which both parties think is rare and valuable, such as Wedgwood Pottery, but which is in fact a fake, they have made a shared mistake which would only render the contract void if the mistake relates to one of three subjects which the courts consider fundamental to the contract: the existence of the subject matter, its ownership and, in limited cases, its quality.

A mistake as to the existence of subject matter will usually only concern goods to be sold-if for example A purports to sell a motorbike to B, and it is then discovered that the motorbike has been destroyed by fire, the contract will not be valid. It can apply equally to other subject matter. The main test is do the goods or other exist at the time of a contract. One case that illustrates this is Scott v Coulson (1993). A life insurance policy was taken out, covering a person's death. In fact the person was already dead so the contract was null and void.

It is not always the case that the non-existence of subject matter will render the contract null and void. There have been several cases which obscure this general principle. One such case was Couturier v Hastie (1856) which involved a contract to buy a cargo of corn, which, at the time the contract was made was supposed to be on a ship sailing to England from the Mediterranean port of Salonica. In fact, by that time the corn had already been sold by the Master of the ship to a buyer in Tunis because the corn had started to deteriorate and go off. This is a common occurrence and the master's action was the usual accepted solution. For the purposes of the original contract the corn had ceased to exist.

The sellers claimed that the buyers still had an obligation to pay as per the contract. The House of Lords held that the buyer did not have to pay for the corn, as the goods did not exist. There was no mistake; quite simply the corn did not exist.

Mistake as to title

Very rarely, a situation will arise in which one party agrees to transfer property to the other but unknown to both parties, the latter already owns that property. In such a case, the contract will be void for mistake. This is obviously very rare but has happened on occasion.

Mistaken identity

There is a presumption that a contract is valid even where one party has made a mistake as to the identity of the other. However, this presumption can be denied or negated by the party who has made the mistake. If this is done the contract is void at common law. In order to achieve this the mistaken party must prove that they intended to deal with a person other than the person who was in fact the other party to the contract, and that the identity of the other party was regarded as of fundamental importance. One key case that illustrates this is Cundy V Lindsey (1878). The claimants received an order for a large number of handkerchiefs from a Mr Blenkarn of 37 Wood street. Cheapside. Mr Blenkarn rented a room at that address, and further down the road at 123 Cheapside, were the offices of a firm called Blenkiron and Co. Blenkarn signed his name so it looked liked Blenkiron. The claimants sent off their goods addressed to Blenkiron and Co. Mr Blenkarn received them and by the time that the fraud was discovered he had sold them to the defendants, Cundy, who had bought them in good faith. The claimants sued the defendants to get the money back, and their success in this depended on whether it could be proved that there was a contract between the claimants and Blenkarn. The House of Lords held that there was no contract between Blenkarn and the claimants, because they had intended all along to deal with Blenkiron and Co. The court very importantly held that 'between him and them there was no consensus of mind which could lead to…any contract whatsoever.

Mistake over the terms of the contract

Where one party is mistaken as to the terms of the contract, and the other knows this, the contract will be void, regardless of whether the term is fundamental.

Mistakes relating to documents

Where a mistake relates to a written document there are two special remedies in existence, non est factum and rectification. Although the general principle is that a contract becomes effective when a person signs it, regardless of whether they understood it, non est factum (this is not my deed) becomes operative where a person signs a document believing it to be something totally different from what it actually was. This remedy may make the contract void. In order to void the contract the person seeking this remedy must prove three things: that the signature was induced by a trick or a fraud, that they made a fundamental mistake as to the nature of the document and that they were not careless in signing it. The mistake made by the signee must concern the actual nature of the contract and not just its legal effect.

Rectification

Where some aspect of a written document is alleged not to reflect accurately the will of the parties, the remedy of rectification may in certain instances allow the written document to be altered so that it coincides with the true agreement of the parties. In order for this remedy to be applied, three conditions must be satisfied: the parties must have agreed about the point in question; the agreement on that aspect of the contract must have continued unchanged up to the time it was put into writing and the written document must fail to express the parties agreement on that point.

Main points from chapter four

- In certain cases, a mistake within a contract can render that contract void. However, the law in this area operates quite rigidly

- There are two types of mistake within contract law – common mistake and cross-purpose mistake

- In order to void the contract the mistake must have been made before the contract was entered into

5

Contracts and Illegality

Although a contract, on the face of it may contain all the elements of a valid agreement, such as offer and consideration, that contract may still be legally unenforceable.

Contracts may be illegal at the time of their formation or because of the way they have been performed. A contract may be illegal when entered into because the contract cannot be performed in accordance with its terms without committing an illegal act. For example, a contract may involve a breach of the criminal law, or it may be a statutory requirement for the parties to the contract to have a licence which they in fact do not have. A case which perfectly illustrates this is Levy v Yates (1838). In this case, there existed a statutory rule that a royal licence was required to perform a play within 20 miles of London. In that case the contract was between a theatre owner and an impresario for the performance of a theatrical production where no royal licence had been obtained. The contract was thus illegal at the time of its formation.

Illegal mode of performance

In some cases a contract may be perfectly legal when it was made, but may be carried out in an illegal manner. A case that illustrates this is Anderson Ltd v Daniel (1924). In this case, a statute provided that a seller of artificial fertiliser had to supply buyers with an invoice detailing certain chemicals used in its manufacture. The sellers failed to provide the invoice needed. Although not against the law to sell fertiliser it was against statutory rules not to supply an invoice. As a result the sellers were unable to claim the price when the defendants refused to pay.

A contract is obviously illegal if it involves a contravention of the law. However, a contract is also regarded as being illegal where it involves conduct which the law disapproves of as contrary to the interests of the public, even though the conduct is not actually unlawful. In both cases the transaction is treated as an illegal contract and the courts will not enforce it.

Contracts violating legal rules

Breach of common law

There are a number of factors which may make a contract illegal at common law, the most important where there is a contract to commit a crime or tort (negligent act) These are obvious breaches of the law. However, another important area is contracts in restraint of trade. The issue of restraint of trade commonly arises and concerns those contracts which limit an individuals rights to use their skills for payment, or to trade freely. These contracts fall into four groups:

- Contracts for the sale of a business where the vendor promises not to compete with the purchaser

- Contracts between businesses by which prices or output are regulated

- Contracts in which an employee agrees that on leaving employment they will not set up in business or be employed in such as way as to compete with their employer or ex

56

- employer. This is most common in business where personal skills and reputation attract custom, such as advertising and the ex-employee may take with them valuable customers

- Contracts where a person agrees to restrict their mode of trade by, for example, only accepting orders from one particular company. This is sometimes called a 'solus' agreement and is frequently used for petrol stations, in return for the land or lease the trader promises to use the product of the seller.

Any of the above can be held to create a restraint of trade, a general restraint if the contract completely prohibits trading, or a partial restraint if it limits trading to a certain time or area.

Breach of legislation

Some types of contract are expressly declared void by statute. The two most important examples of contracts that are expressly declared void by statute are contracts in constraint of trade and wagering contracts.

Competition law

Common law lays down certain controls on contracts in constraint of trade. These controls give only limited protection and actual legislation provides more adequate protection. One of the main goals of the European Union, through Article 85, is to promote free trade between member states and clearly restrictive trade can affect this policy. Where a restrictive trade agreement could affect trade between member states it will only be valid if allowed under both EU and English law. In terms of contracts in English law, the relevant legislation is now contained in the Competition Act 1998. This Act prohibits a number of anti-competitive practices. The 1998 Act applies to agreements between undertakings, decisions by associations of undertakings or concerted practices which (a) may affect trade and (b) have as their object or effect the prevention, restriction or distortion of trade. For the Act to prohibit an agreement the effect of the agreement must be significant and not minor.

Wagering contracts

Wagering agreements are bets, and are rendered void by the Gaming Act 1845. Section 18 of the Act provides:

All contracts or agreements, whether by parole or in writing, by way of gaming or wagering, shall be null and void, and no suit shall be brought or maintained in a court of law or equity for recovering any sum of money or valuable thing alleged to be won upon any wager…

The Act does not make wagering agreements illegal, it simply provides that neither party to such an agreement can legally enforce it. For the provisions of the legislation to apply, a wagering contract must be one in which there are two parties and the terms of the agreement are such that one party wins and the other loses. This means that football pools, for example, are not covered as its promoters take a percentage of the stake money and so gain by the transaction regardless of whether players win as well. The Act also covers gaming, which is defined by the Betting, Gaming and lotteries act 1963 as 'the playing of a game of chance for winnings in money or money's worth'. Games of chance include games which depend partly on skill and partly on chance. Athletic games and sports are excluded.

Contracts against public policy

There are a range of contracts which are considered to be illegal because they are against public policy. As we discussed, public policy really means the interest of society at large and the contract must contravene it. Contracts promoting sexual immorality for example are seen as contravening public policy. One case that illustrates this is Armhouse Lee Ltd v Chappell (1996) which concerned a contract under which the defendants paid the plaintiffs to place adverts for telephone sex lines in magazines. When regulation concerning such publicity was tightened the defendants terminated the contract as they no longer wished to advertise their services in this way. The plaintiffs brought an action for the money due under the contract, the defendants argued that the contract was illegal and unenforceable as it promoted sexual immorality. This defence was rejected by the Court of Appeal. The court held that though the adverts were distasteful the sex lines were generally accepted by society and were regulated by the telephone industry. There was no evidence, in the eyes of the Court of Appeal that any 'generally accepted moral code' condemned these telephone sex lines. It considered that contracts should only be found illegal under this heading if an element of public harm clearly existed.

Contracts prejudicial to public safety

The main types of contracts found illegal on these grounds are contracts with those living in an enemy country, contracts to perform acts which are illegal in a friendly foreign country and contracts which are damaging to foreign relations.

The effect of an illegal contract

The effect of an illegal contract will depend on whether it is illegal due to a statute or due to the common law. Where the contract is illegal due to a statute, in some cases the statute provides for the consequences of any illegality. Under common law an illegal contract is void and courts will not order it to be performed.

The precise effects of an illegal contract depend on whether the contract is illegal at the time of formation or is illegal due to the way in which it was performed.

Contracts illegal at the time of formation are treated as if they were never made, so the illegal contract is unenforceable by either party. Contracts illegal as performed are slightly different as to their effect. It will be possible to enforce the illegal contract if the illegal act was merely incidental to the performance of the contract. For example, a contract for the delivery of goods may not be tainted by illegality when the lorry driver is caught speeding or under the influence of drink.

Where the contract is merely illegal because of the way it was performed, it is possible for either both or only one of the parties to intend illegal performance. If both parties are aware that a contracts performance is illegal, the consequences for this type of contract are the same as for a contract that was illegal at the time of its formation. When one party did not know of the illegal performance of the contract by the other party, the innocent party can enforce it.

In some cases, it is possible to divide the illegal part of a contract from the rest and enforce the provisions which are not affected by the illegality-this is called severance. The illegal parts of the contract can be severed if they are relatively unimportant to the contract and if the severance leaves the nature of the contract unaltered.

Main points from chapter five

- Although a contract may contain all the elements of a valid agreement, such as offer and consideration, that contract may still not be legally enforceable.

- Contracts may be illegal at the time of their formation or because of the way they have been performed.

- In some cases, a contract may be perfectly legal when made, but may be carried out in an illegal manner

- Contracts may breach common law, legislation, competition law or public policy

6

Duress and Undue Influence

As we have seen, contracts are only binding if parties voluntarily consent to them. If one party is forced to sign under duress, the contract is invalid. As is usual, the law has developed two doctrines to deal with duress: the common law of duress and the equitable one of undue influence.

Duress

Although traditionally, common law has dealt with duress in terms of physical or psychological duress exerted when signing a contract, the doctrine has now been extended to economic duress. This, as the term implies, is where one party is forced into the contract due to economic pressure. Economic duress first arose in North Ocean Shipping Co v Hyundai Construction Co (The Atlantic Baron) (1979) which concerned a contract for the building of a ship. As is commonly the case where duress is raised, the dispute concerned not the formation of the contract, but a supposed modification of its terms. Such a modification can only be binding if both parties consent to it. If one party's consent is achieved by duress the contract is void.

Although the price of the ship had been fixed at the outset` while it was being built the sellers decided to raise the price by ten per cent, due to a drop in the exchange rate of the dollar. The buyers were not happy about this but were unwilling to risk delaying completion of the ship as they were already negotiating for it to be chartered by a major oil company. They therefore agreed to pay the increased price.

Eight months after the ship was delivered the buyers tried to sue the sellers claiming back the ten per cent because they said that it had been extracted from them under duress. The judge agreed that economic power constituted duress, the question being whether there had been 'compulsion of will'. This compulsion could stem from economic pressure as well as physical force. In this particular case the buyers were not allowed to recover the extra ten per cent. This was not because duress did not play a part as it did, but that they waited so long after delivery to sue, implying acceptance.

Economic duress will be present where there is compulsion of will to the extent that the party under threat has no practical alternative but to comply, and the pressure used is regarded by the law as illegitimate.

Undue influence

Undue influence is an equitable doctrine, which applies where one party uses their influence over another to persuade them to make a contract. Where a court finds that a contract was made as a result of undue influence, it may set it aside, or modify its terms. There are two types of undue influence: actual and presumed.

Actual undue influence arises where the claimant can prove that they entered into the transaction as a result of undue influence from the other party. An example is where a person promises to either pay money or give goods in exchange for a promise not to report them for a criminal offence. The party claiming duress must prove that they were influenced.

Presumed undue influence will arise where there is a pre-existing relationship between the parties to a contract, as a result of which one places trust in another, and the contract between them is obviously disadvantageous to the one placing trust in another. Such a relationship of trust is called a fiduciary relationship and it may arise in two ways. It may fall into a category in which a relationship of trust is presumed to exist, such as patient-doctor, solicitor and client and so on. Where a relationship does not fall into obvious categories then a relationship of trust may well be established through, for example, effluxion of time or inherent trust such as an ongoing successful business relationship.

One example of a fiduciary relationship is in the case of Lloyds Bank v Bundy (1974). The plaintiff and his son both used the same bank. The son ran into business difficulties and the father was asked to guarantee the overdraft. He did this, putting up his farm as a guarantee and the bank tried to repossess the farm. The farmer claimed that the contract had been obtained by undue influence, on the basis that he had banked with Lloyds for a long time, and in that time had placed considerable trust in their advice, yet they had made no effort to warn him that it was not in their interest to give the guarantee. The Court of Appeal agreed that the presumption of undue influence had been raised. There was a relationship based on trust over time and the bank lost the case.

The transaction must be extremely disadvantageous (manifestly so) to give rise to a presumption of undue influence. This will be the case where it would have been 'obvious to any independent and reasonable persons who considered the transaction at that time with knowledge of all the relevant facts'. (Bank of Credit and Commerce International SA v Aboody (1989)).

Inequality of bargaining power

In Lloyds Bank v Bundy, as described above, Lord Denning suggested that economic duress was simply an example of a general principle of inequality of bargaining power. He argued that this principle allows English law to give relief to anyone who, without taking independent advice, makes a contract on unfair terms, or sells property for much less than it is worth because their own bargaining power is seriously compromised by ignorance, infirmity or need. Clearly, this is a key principle when negotiating and entering into contracts, more pertinent than simple undue influence as there is no suggestion that the other party had behaved improperly.

Main points from chapter Six

- Contracts are only binding if the parties to that contract voluntary consent to the terms

- If one party is forced to sign under duress the contract can be void

- Duress can be physical, psychological or economic

7

Rights of Third Parties

A third party to any contract is a person who is not a party to the contract and has not provided consideration for the contract but has an interest in the performance. There has been a rule, long established in contract law, that only the parties to the contract could incur rights and obligations under it. This is known as 'privity of contract' this principle meaning that third parties could neither sue nor be sued under the contract.

There are two main aspects to the rule of privity. The first is that the third party cannot be made the subject of a burden imposed by the contract. The second is that a third party cannot enforce a benefit purported to be granted by the contract. This second rule has been heavily criticised, as it is inherently unjust and can lead to hardship and resulted in much debate and eventual reform leading to the Contracts (Rights of Third Parties) Act 1999. The privity rule has now only very limited effect. The Act has made changes in the way that contracts can be enforced by third parties.

The rights of third parties

The Contract (Rights of Third Parties) Act 1999 enables third parties to enforce contractual terms in certain situations. The Act applies to contracts made on or after 11th May 2000 or to contracts made during the six-month period after Royal Assent (11th November 1999) if the contract expressly states that the Act applies. Under the Act, third parties can sue in two situations:

-the contract expressly provides that they may do so; or
-the contract purports to confer a benefit on them, unless it is clear
-that the term was not intended to be enforceable by the third party.

Express provision in the contract
Section 1 of the Act deals with this area. This enables the parties to expressly identify the third party in the contract.

The contract purports to confer a benefit on a third party
This is subject to an important provision that it will not apply if the contract expressly outlines this. The contract must specifically state that third parties will not benefit. In the absence of this then there may be a purported benefit to a third party inherent in the contract.

Under either of the above it is not necessary for the third party to be named. Nor need the person be in existence at the time of the contracts formation. The Act also provides that third parties are able to rely on a contracts exclusion or limitation clauses which are intended to cover them.

Consent to variations
The rights conferred under the Act would be of limited value if the contracting parties could at any time change their minds and remove the promised benefit. Section 2 of the act deals with the issue of amending and canceling contracts. The section states that unless the contract states otherwise, the parties to the contract may not rescind the contract, or vary it, so as to extinguish the third parties rights without their consent if the third party has either:

-communicated to the promisor their assent to the relevant term;
-relied on that term and the promisor knows of that reliance; or

-relied on the term and the promisor can reasonably be expected to have foreseen that reliance.

If one of these three situations applies, then any variations or cancellations can only take place with the consent of the third party.

Third parties to a contract have remedies that are available to them as if they were contracting parties.

Common law exceptions

Agency

The term 'agent' has a specific meaning in this context, and applies to an individual who makes a contract on behalf of someone else who is know as the principal. In the contract sense, an agent is viewed by the law as an intermediary of the principal, rather than a true party to the contract. In practice, one party to a contract made by an agent is usually a corporation of one kind or another, such as a PLC or a Local Authority, and the agent is their employee.

There are three circumstances in which a party will be treated as an agent: where there is express authority; where there is implied authority; and where there is apparent authority. Express authority means that the agent has specifically asked the agent to make the contract in question. Implied authority arises where the agent is asked to do something where by implication a contract is to be made. Apparent authority is more problematic and arises where the principals past behaviour gives the party to the contract reason to believe that the agent has authority to contract on the agent's behalf.

Assignment

It is possible to assign the benefit of the contract without the permission of the other party. A common example is where a small business with cash flow problems sells the debts owed to them to others who are factoring businesses.

Collateral contracts

Where one party makes contracts with two others, the courts will sometimes use the device of 'finding' a collateral contract between the two others to evade the privity rule. An example of this is Shanklin Pier Ltd v Detel Products Ltd (1951). The plaintiffs owned Shanklin Pier, and needed it repainting. They contracted Detel to inquire about the qualities of its paint, and were told that it lasted between 7-10 years. The plaintiffs employed other contractors and told them to use Detel paint. The paint started to peel after three months and the Plaintiffs could not sue the contractors as it was not they who had stated that the paint would last 7-10 years. The pier owners had no contract with Detel since the paint was bought by the contractors. However, the court held that there was in fact a collateral contract between the pier owners and Detel as Detel had told them that the paint would last, and the Pier owners request that the painters should use Detel paint was collateral for that promise.

Key points from chapter seven

- A third party to any contract is a person who is not party to the contract and has not provided consideration for the contract but has an interest in the performance

- The long established rulke has been that only the parties to the contract could incur rights and obligations under it. This is known as 'privity of contract, this principle meaning that third parties could neither sue nor be sued under the contract

- This longstanding rule has been amended through The Contract (Rights of Third Parties Act) 1999 that enables third parties to enforce contractual terms in certain situations. In addition those who are party to the contract cam bring an action against the third party.

8

Discharge of Terms of a Contract

A contract is said to be discharged when the rights and obligations in it come to an end. There are four ways in which a contract can come to an end: performance under the contract, i.e., natural end, end by mutual agreement, breach of contract and frustration. We should look at these areas in turn.

Performance under contract

This is the most obvious way of parties discharging their obligations and bringing the contract to a satisfactory end. In many cases, it is uncomplicated but there are some cases where one party may claim to have discharged their obligations and the other party disagrees. The law then has to look at the question of what constitutes performance.

The obvious and general rule is that performance must exactly match the requirements laid down in the contract. This is known as entire performance. If the first party fails to perform then the other party need pay nothing at all, even if the shortfall actually causes no hardship. This is the simple rule and obviously contracts can be more complicated, with claim and counter claim.

The case of Cutter v Powell (1795) demonstrates the difficulty. A sailor had contracted to serve on a ship travelling from Jamaica to Liverpool. He was to be paid 30 Guineas for the voyage, payable when the ship arrived in Liverpool. However, he died during the journey. His widow sued for wages up until he died, but her claim was unsuccessful, as the court held that the contract required entire performance.

The rule can also allow parties to escape from what has become an unprofitable contract to do so by taking advantage of the most minor departures from its terms. In Re Moore and Co Ltd and Landaur and Co (1921) the contract concerned the sale of canned fruits which were to be packed into cases of 30 tins. On delivery it was discovered that although the correct number of tins had been sent, almost half the cases contained only 24 tins in each. This made no difference to the market value of the goods, but the buyers pointed out that the sale was covered by the Sale of Goods Act, which stated that goods sold by description must correspond with that description. The delivery did not, and the buyers were within their rights to reject the whole consignment.

Mitigation of the entire performance rule

Substantial performance
This doctrine allows a party who has performed with only minor defects to claim the price of the work done, less any money the other party will have to spend to put the defects right.

Severable contracts
A contract is said to be severable where payment becomes due at various stages of performance, rather than in one lump sum when performance is complete. Most contracts of employment are examples of this. Also, major building contracts also operate in this way, allowing for stage payments. In a severable contract the money due at the end of each stage may be claimed and the person carrying out the work under the contract can refuse to continue if the payments are not made.

Prevention of performance by one party

Where one party performs one part of the agreed obligation, and is then prevented from completing the rest of the contract because of a fault of the other party, a quantum meruit can be claimed from the other party. Quantum meruit is an assessment of the amount performed to date and a reasonable price arrived at.

Breach of terms concerning time

The judgment here will be that of an assessment of whether 'time is of the essence' and the effect that completing the contract out of time has on the other party.

Frustration of contract

The basic principle underlying frustration of contract is that, after a contract is made, something happens, through no fault of the parties own, to make fulfillment of the contract impossible. Although there are many situations which can make it impossible to fulfill a contract only certain cases can be seen as genuine frustration.

The modern doctrine of frustration arose from Taylor v Caldwell (1863). The parties in the case had entered into an agreement concerning the use of Surrey Gardens and music hall for a series of concerts and day and night fetes. Six days before the planned date for the first concert, the building was burnt down, making it impossible for the concerts to go ahead. The party planning to put on the concerts was sued for breach of contract but the action failed as fulfillment of the contract was impossible.

The concept and practice of frustration of contract can be placed in three categories: events which make performance or further performance impossible; events which make performance illegal; and those which make it pointless.

Impossible to fulfill contract

A contract may become impossible to perform because of destruction or unavailability of something essential for the contract to be performed.

Death of either party to the contract

Unavailability of party. Contracts which require personal performance will be frustrated if one party, for example, is ill or is imprisoned, providing that the non-availability of the party substantially effects performance

Method of performance impossible

Where a contract lays down a particular method of performance and this becomes impossible, the contract may be frustrated.

A contract is unlikely to be frustrated simply because performance has become more expensive or more onerous than expected. The leading modern case on frustration is Davis Contractors Co Ltd v Fareham UDC (1956). Davis, a construction company contracted to build 78 houses for a local authority. The job was to take eight months, at a price of £94,000. In fact, labour shortages delayed the work, which ended up taking 22 months and cost the builders £22,000 more than they had planned for. The defendant was willing to pay the contract price in spite of the delay, but Davis sought to have the contract discharged on the grounds of frustration arguing that labour shortages made performance fundamentally different from that envisaged in the contract (it intended to seek payment on a quantum meruit basis to cover costs).

However, the House of Lords decided that the events which caused the delays were within the range of changes which could reasonably be expected to happen during the performance of a contract for building houses and the change of circumstances did not make performance radically different from what was expected. Therefore, the contract was not frustrated. Lord Radcliffe explained:

'it is not hardship or inconvenience or material loss which itself calls the principle of frustration into play. There must be as well such a change in the significance of the obligation that the thing undertaken would, if performed, be different from that contracted for'.

Illegality
If, after a contract is formed, a change in the law makes its performance illegal, the contract will be frustrated.

Performance made pointless
A contract can be frustrated where a supervening event makes performance of a contract completely pointless, though still technically possible. A contract can be rendered pointless if there has been such a drastic change of circumstances as to dramatically alter the nature of the contract.

Time of frustrating event
In order to frustrate a contract, the event in question must occur after the contract is made.

Breach of contract
A contract is said to be breached when one party performs defectively, or differently from the agreement or not at all (actual breach) or indicates in advance that they will not be performing as agreed (anticipatory breach). Where an anticipatory breach occurs,

the other party can sue for breach straight away, it is not necessary to wait until performance falls due. One case illustrating this is Frost v Knight (1872) where the defendant had promised to marry the plaintiff once his father had died. He later broke off the engagement before his father died, and when his ex-fiance sued him for breach of promise, he argued that she had no claim as the time for performance had not yet arrived. This argument was rejected and the plaintiff's case succeeded.

Any effect of a breach of contract will entitle the innocent party to sue for damages but not every breach will entitle the wronged party to discharge the contract. If the contract is not discharged it will still need to be performed. There are three main circumstances where the innocent party may wish to seek to discharge the contract:

Repudiation – this is where one party makes it clear that they no longer wish to be bound by the contract, either during its performance or before performance is due

Breach of a condition – Breach of a condition allows the innocent party to terminate the contract.

Serious breach of an innominate term – where the relevant term is classified as innominate, it will be the one that can be breached in both serious and trivial ways, and whether the innocent party is entitled to terminate or not will depend on how serious the results of the breach are. If the results are so serious as to undermine the foundations of the contract, the innocent party will have the right to terminate.

Even when one of these three types of breach occurs, the contract is not automatically discharged. The innocent party can usually choose whether or not to terminate. If the innocent party chooses to terminate this must be clearly communicated to the other party.

Agreement

In some cases, the parties to a contract will simply agree to terminate the contract, so that one or both parties are released from their obligations. A distinction is usually made between bilateral discharge where both parties will benefit from the ending by agreement and a unilateral discharge where one party benefits.

In general an agreed discharge will be binding if it contains the same elements that make a contract binding when it is formed. The two which present the most problems are formality and consideration.

Consideration

Consideration is not usually a problem where both parties agree to alter their obligations since each is giving something in return for the change. Problems are most likely to occur when one parties obligations change. If the other party agrees to the change, their agreement will only be binding if put into the form of a deed, or supported by consideration. Where consideration is provided in return for one party's agreement to change this is called 'accord'. The provision of consideration is called 'satisfaction'. The arrangement is often termed accord and satisfaction.

Formalities

This issue arises in connection with certain types of contract (mainly concerning the sale of land) which must be evidenced in writing to be binding under the Law of Property Act (1925).

Remedies for breach of contract

There are a number of remedies available to the innocent party in the event of a breached contract. There are two main remedies, those under common law and equitable remedies. There is a third category which involves remedies arising from the parties own agreement.

Main points from chapter Eight

- A contract is said to be discharged when the rights and obligations in it come to an end. There are four ways in which a contract can come to an end – performance under the contract, end by mutual agreement, breach of contract and frustration

- A contract can be frustrated, the basic principle being that, after a contract has been made something happens through no fault of any party then the contract can be voided through frustration of its terms

- Contracts can be deemed to be frustrated on death

9

Common Law Remedies for Breach of Contract

The usual remedy for breach of contracts is the award of damages to the innocent party. It aims to compensate for losses that result from not receiving performance that was due under the contract. In general the damages will cover both physical harm to the claimant and their property and also for any economic loss. There are very limited circumstances in which injury to feelings can be compensated for.

When considering damages the general rule is that any damages are awarded innocent parties will place them in a position they would have been if the contract had been performed. There are, however, three limitations,: causation, remoteness and mitigation.

Causation

A person will be liable only for losses caused by their own breach of contract. Acts intervening between the breach of contract and the loss incurred may break the chain of causation. One case illustrating this is County Ltd v Girozentrale Securities (1996) where the plaintiff's bank agreed to underwrite the issue of 26 million shares in a publicly quoted company. The defendants were stockbrokers who were engaged by the plaintiffs to approach potential investors in the shares. The brokers breached the terms of their contract and, in due course, the plaintiffs found themselves with 4.5 million shares on their hands which, the price of shares having fallen, represented a loss of nearly £7.5m. They sued the stockbrokers and the main issue in the case was whether the plaintiff's loss was caused by the defendant's breach of contract. In effect the plaintiffs would not have suffered their loss if there had not been a concurrence of a number of events of which the defendants breach of contract was one. The Court of Appeal held that the brokers breach of contract remained the effective cause of the plaintiffs loss, the breach did not need to be the only cause. The defendants were liable for damages.

Remoteness

There are some losses which clearly result from the defendant's breach of contract, but are considered too remote from the breach for compensation to arise.

The rules concerning remoteness were originally laid down in Hadley v Baxendale (1854). The case concerned a contract for delivery of an important piece of mill equipment, which had been sent away for repair. The equipment, an iron shaft, was not delivered until some days after the agreed date, which meant that the mill, which could not work without it, stood idle for the period whilst awaiting the part. The mill owners attempted to sue for this loss. The courts held that the defendant could not be liable for the loss in this case.

Mitigation

Claimants cannot simply sit back, do nothing, and let losses pile up and expect compensation for the whole loss if there was something that could have been done to mitigate the loss. It is up to defendants in this case to prove that the loss could have been mitigated. Claimants need only do what is reasonable to mitigate the loss.

Calculating any loss

Once it has been established that there is a loss and the defendant is liable the court must quantify the damages. In 1936, two American academics, Fuller and Perdue came up with two main ways of calculating compensation:

Loss of expectation (also called loss of bargain). This is the usual way in which contract damages are calculated and it aims to put claimants in the position that they would have been if the contract had not been performed.

Reliance loss. There are some cases of loss that are very difficult to quantify and in this case, the court may award damages calculated to compensate for any expenses or other loss incurred by the claimant when relying on the contract.

Action for an agreed sum

Where a contract specifies a price to be paid for performance, and the party due to pay fails to do so, the party who has performed can claim the price owing by means of an action for the agreed sum. Although the claim is for money this is not the same as a claim for damages. The claimant is not seeking compensation, but simply enforcement of the defendants promise to pay. However, where the claimant has suffered additional loss beyond not receiving the agreed price, damages can be claimed alongside the agreed sum. An action such as this can only be brought once the duty to pay has arisen

Restitution

Where money has been paid under a contract or purported contract and performance has not been received in return, or has not been adequate, the payer may want to claim the money back, rather than claiming damages (if, for example, no additional loss has resulted from the failure to perform). In general this will only be possible if there has been a total failure of consideration so that restitution will prevent undue enrichment. This means that the party paying the money has not received any of what was paid for.

Equitable remedies

Where common law remedies are inadequate to compensate the claimant, there is a range of equitable remedies. However, these are not available as of right, merely because the defendant is in breach. They are provided at the discretion of the court, taking into account the behavior of both parties and the overall circumstances.

Specific performance

The common law will not force a specific party in breach to perform (except where performance is paying money only), even though this might be a fairly obvious solution to many contract problems. However, the equitable remedy of specific performance does compel a party in breach to perform. In practice, specific performance rarely applies as the making of such an order is subject to certain restrictions.

Specific performance is only granted if damages alone would be an inadequate remedy Specific performance is mainly applied to contracts to sell land since each piece of land is thought to be unique and impossible to replace. Where the damages are only nominal specific performance may be ordered to stop one party becoming unjustly enriched.

Because specific performance is a discretionary remedy the court will not apply it to cases where it could cause the claimant great hardship or unfairness.

The courts will also allow the courts to refuse specific

performance of a contract which has been obtained by unfair means.

Some type of contract are unsuitable for specific performance, the two main types being contracts involving personal services (such as employment contracts) and contracts which involve continuous duties.

Injunctions

Another remedy is that of the injunction. An injunction orders the defendant not to do a specific thing. Where the contract has already been breached the courts can make a mandatory injunction which will order the defendant to restore the situation to what it was before the breach.

Remedies agreed by the parties

Many contracts specify the kind of breach which will justify termination and the damages to be paid. There are two types of contractual clauses concerning damages: liquidated damages and penalty clauses.

Liquidated damages is the term used where a contract specifies the amount of damages to be paid in the event of a breach, and this amount represents a genuine attempt to work out what the loss in the event if such a breach would be.

Penalty damages work in a different way. Some contracts, especially construction contracts, specify very high damages in the event of breach and they act as a deterrent, compelling the other party to perform. Where a court finds the damages laid down in contract act in this way, the relevant clause will be invalid and the party putting forward the clause must pursue damages in the usual way.

One case which illustrates this, and which provided for guidelines was that of Dunlop Pneumatic Tyre Co Ltd v New

Garage and Motor Co Ltd (1915). The plaintiffs supplied tyres to the defendants under a contract providing that the defendants would not resell them at less than the list price. If they breached this provision they would be liable to pay £5 for every tyre sold at less than the list price.

The House of Lords held that the provision was not penal and was in the nature of liquidated damages. Undercutting the list price would have been damaging to the plaintiffs business.

Lord Dunedin described the factors to be taken into account when deciding whether damages were penal or not, damages would be considered penal if the sum laid down was extravagantly greater than any loss that might conceivably result from the breach.

Main points from chapter nine

- The usual remedy for breach of contracts is the award of damages to the innocent party

- When considering damages the general rule is that any damages that are awarded innocent parties will place them in a position that they would have been if the contract had performed

- Losses can be mitigated

- Parties can seek specific performance under the contract

- Parties can also apply for an injunction to force the other party to perform.

Glossary of terms

The following are common terms encountered when dealing with contracts.

Acceptance (of an offer) agreement to al the terms of a contract. Can be oral or in writing.

Accord and satisfaction – this occurs where one party's obligations under a contract change and consideration is provided in return for the other party's agreement to the change.

Agent – a person authorized to act on behalf of another who is known to the main party to the contract

Bilateral contract – where each party takes on an obligation, usually for promising the other something

Breach of a contract – where one party does not perform, or performs differently from the agreement

Condition – a term in a contract which is an important term and a breach of this term would have significant consequences to one party

Consideration – something that must be provided by each of the parties in order to make a binding contract

Contract – a legally binding agreement, written or unwritten

Cross purpose mistake – where each party to the contract has a different view of the contractual situation

Economic duress – where one party is forced into a contract due to economic pressure

Exclusion clause – a clause which tries to exclude all responsibility for certain breaches of contract

Freedom of contract – promotes the idea that parties should be allowed to bargain without interference from the courts

Implied terms – terms which are not expressly used in a contract but which can be read into the contract

Indemnity clause – provides that one party will reimburse the other in the event of any loss arising from the contract

Innominate terms – these are terms that can be broken with either important or trivial consequences, depending ion the nature of the breach

Limitation clause – this is where either party to the contract will seek to limit their liability for any loss

Liquidated damages – this is where a contract specifies the amount of damages to be paid in the event of a breach

Misrepresentation – where one party is induced to enter into a contract as a result of false statement of another

Offer – this is where communication is treated as an offer if it indicates the terms on which the offeror is prepared to make a contract and gives a clear indication that the offeror intends to be bound by the terms of the contract

Privity of contract – this is where that only the parties to the contract incur rights and obligations under it

Quantum meruit – where a price has not been specified under a contract between parties but work has been done and a reasonable price can be claimed

Severable contract – this is where a contract can be severed where payment becomes due at various stages of performance rather than in one lump sum

Subject to contract – parties do not intend to be bound by law until formal contracts are exchanged

Terms of the contract – these describe the duties and obligations which each party has under the agreement

Unilateral contracts – arises where only one party assumes an obligation

Void contract – this is where a contract is declared void, the effect being that there never was a contract in the first place

Voidable contract – this is where an innocent party to the contract can chose to terminate it

Warranty – this describes a contractual term which can be

broken without highly important consequences. If a warranty is breached, the innocent party can sue for damages but cannot terminate the contract.

Index